STUMME, ABSOLON
The Tree of Jesse
(tempera on panel)
Hamburger Kunsthalle, Hamburg, Germany

The Illustrated Life of Jesus of Nazareth

*Drawn from the Gospel Accounts
and the Works of Great Artists*

Introduction by James Underhill

KONECKY&KONECKY

Konecky & Konecky
72 Ayers Point Rd.
Old Saybrook, CT 06475

Copyright © 2014 by Konecky & Konecky, LLC.

All pictures courtesy of the Bridgeman Images

ISBN: 978-1-56852-811-3

Please visit us on the web at www.koneckyandkonecky.com

Printed in China

Introduction

James Underhill

The good news of salvation of all humankind through the grace of our Lord Jesus Christ is announced by Luke and then confirmed by John. The synoptic Gospel accounts of Matthew, Mark and Luke tell the story of Jesus' ministry, crucifixion and resurrection. The Gospel of John expands on their accounts, providing a profound meditation on the nature of Christ and his mission to the world.

One essential component of Jesus' message is its rootedness in the Old Testament, the scriptures of the Jewish people. As he himself says: "Think not that I am come to destroy the law, or the prophets: I am not come to destroy, but to fulfil. " (Matthew 5:17). Jesus' first words, in answer to his mother, who has asked him where he has been, are "How is it that you sought me? Did you not know that I must be in my Father's house?" (Luke 2: 49), that is, in the temple. And according to Matthew his last words on the cross are "Eli, Eli, lama sabachthani," which is an Aramaic translation of the first line of Psalm 22 (My God, my God, why hast Thou forsaken me?). Jesus' discourses abound in citations of Old Testament texts, and in using parables he employed a teaching method common to the Jewish moralists of his day. So we see that Jesus was steeped in the learning and teaching of the Jewish scriptures. Much of his teaching will be difficult to fully understand without a familiarity with the Law of Moses.

But Jesus offers a radically new dispensation. He makes this clear in the parable of wineskins: "Neither do men put new wine into old bottles: else the bottles break, and the wine runneth out, and the bottles perish: but they put new wine into new bottles, and both are preserved" (Matthew 9: 17). He does not nullify the Law but rather uses it as an instrument to accomplish salvation and draw humankind to the Heavenly Father. Upon his coming into the world, the Law no longer is sufficient. It is for this reason that Paul teaches us:

Be it known unto you therefore, men and brethren, that through this man is preached unto you the forgiveness of sins:

And by him all that believe are justified from all things, from which ye could not be justified by the law of Moses.

(Acts 13: 38–39)

For Jesus ransomed us through his blood and death on the cross that we may enjoy the fullness of grace and be numbered among the children of the ever-living God.

In this book we tell the story of Jesus' life through the words of the Gospels and works of art created in the centuries since his time on earth. They range from a Byzantine mosaic of the twelfth century depicting Jesus healing a leper, to a contemporary interpretation of the Massacre of the Innocents. Inspired by devotion, painters and other artists have bequeathed to us a pictorial biography from the Annunciation to the Resurrection and Ascension. The art that Jesus inspired must rank as the pinnacle of creative achievement. In his role as intermediary between God and man, the Word made flesh, the figure of Christ has provided artists with an opportunity to reach for their highest idealizations, while at the same time compassionate for human suffering which he took upon himself.

RAPHAEL
The Alba Madonna
(c.1510) (oil on panel)
National Gallery of Art, Washington DC

The Annunciation
Luke 1

26 And in the sixth month the angel Gabriel was sent from God unto a city of Galilee, named Nazareth,

27 To a virgin espoused to a man whose name was Joseph, of the house of David; and the virgin's name was Mary.

28 And the angel came in unto her, and said, Hail, thou that art highly favoured, the LORD is with thee: blessed art thou among women.

29 And when she saw him, she was troubled at his saying, and cast in her mind what manner of salutation this should be.

30 And the angel said unto her, Fear not, Mary: for thou hast found favour with God.

31 And, behold, thou shalt conceive in thy womb, and bring forth a son, and shalt call his name JESUS.

32 He shall be great, and shall be called the Son of the Highest: and the Lord God shall give unto him the throne of his father David:

33 And he shall reign over the house of Jacob for ever; and of his kingdom there shall be no end.

34 Then said Mary unto the angel, How shall this be, seeing I know not a man?

35 And the angel answered and said unto her, The Holy Ghost shall come upon thee, and the power of the Highest shall overshadow thee: therefore also that holy thing which shall be born of thee shall be called the Son of God.

36 And, behold, thy cousin Elisabeth, she hath also conceived a son in her old age: and this is the sixth month with her, who was called barren.

37 For with God nothing shall be impossible.

38 And Mary said, Behold the handmaid of the Lord; be it unto me according to thy word. And the angel departed from her.

CHIESA, PIETRO
The Annunciation
(oil on canvas)
Galleria Nazionale d'Arte Moderna, Rome, Italy

DAVID, GERARD
The Annunciation
Stadelsches Kunstinstitut, Frankfurt-am-Main, Germany

Mary in the House of Elizabeth

Luke 1

39 And Mary arose in those days, and went into the hill country with haste, into a city of Juda;

40 And entered into the house of Zacharias, and saluted Elisabeth.

41 And it came to pass, that, when Elisabeth heard the salutation of Mary, the babe leaped in her womb; and Elisabeth was filled with the Holy Ghost:

42 And she spake out with a loud voice, and said, Blessed art thou among women, and blessed is the fruit of thy womb.

43 And whence is this to me, that the mother of my Lord should come to me?

44 For, lo, as soon as the voice of thy salutation sounded in mine ears, the babe leaped in my womb for joy.

45 And blessed is she that believed: for there shall be a performance of those things which were told her from the Lord.

BELL, ROBERT ANNING
Mary in the House of Elizabeth
1917 (oil on canvas)
Private Collection

THE NAMING OF JOHN THE BAPTIST

Luke 1

57 Now Elisabeth's full time came that she should be delivered; and she brought forth a son.

58 And her neighbours and her cousins heard how the Lord had shewed great mercy upon her; and they rejoiced with her.

59 And it came to pass, that on the eighth day they came to circumcise the child; and they called him Zacharias, after the name of his father.

60 And his mother answered and said, Not so; but he shall be called John.

61 And they said unto her, There is none of thy kindred that is called by this name.

62 And they made signs to his father, how he would have him called.

63 And he asked for a writing table, and wrote, saying, His name is John. And they marvelled all.

64 And his mouth was opened immediately, and his tongue loosed, and he spake, and praised God.

65 And fear came on all that dwelt round about them: and all these sayings were noised abroad throughout all the hill country of Judaea.

66 And all they that heard them laid them up in their hearts, saying, What manner of child shall this be! And the hand of the Lord was with him.

ANGELICO, FRA (GUIDO DI PIETRO)
The Naming of John the Baptist
c.1430s (tempera on panel)
Museo di San Marco dell'Angelico, Florence, Italy

THE NATIVITY
Luke 2

1   And it came to pass in those days, that there went out a decree from Caesar Augustus that all the world should be taxed.

2   (And this taxing was first made when Cyrenius was governor of Syria.)

3   And all went to be taxed, every one into his own city.

4   And Joseph also went up from Galilee, out of the city of Nazareth, into Judaea, unto the city of David, which is called Bethlehem; (because he was of the house and lineage of David:)

5   To be taxed with Mary his espoused wife, being great with child.

6   And so it was, that, while they were there, the days were accomplished that she should be delivered.

7   And she brought forth her firstborn son, and wrapped him in swaddling clothes, and laid him in a manger; because there was no room for them in the inn.

MEMLING, HANS
Nativity Scene
Private Collection

THE ANNUNCIATION TO THE SHEPHERDS

Luke 2

8 And there were in the same country shepherds abiding in the field, keeping watch over their flock by night.

9 And, lo, the angel of the Lord came upon them, and the glory of the Lord shone round about them: and they were sore afraid.

10 And the angel said unto them, Fear not: for, behold, I bring you good tidings of great joy, which shall be to all people.

11 For unto you is born this day in the city of David a Saviour, which is Christ the Lord.

12 And this shall be a sign unto you; Ye shall find the babe wrapped in swaddling clothes, lying in a manger.

13 And suddenly there was with the angel a multitude of the heavenly host praising God, and saying,

14 Glory to God in the highest, and on earth peace, good will toward men.

PIETRO, SANO DI, ALSO ANSANO DI PIETRO DI MENCIO
The Annunciation to the Shepherds
(oil on panel)
Pinacoteca Nazionale, Siena, Italy

THE ADORATION OF THE MAGI

Matthew 2

1   Now when Jesus was born in Bethlehem of Judaea in the days of Herod the king, behold, there came wise men from the east to Jerusalem,

2   Saying, Where is he that is born King of the Jews? for we have seen his star in the east, and are come to worship him.

3   When Herod the king had heard these things, he was troubled, and all Jerusalem with him.

4   And when he had gathered all the chief priests and scribes of the people together, he demanded of them where Christ should be born.

5   And they said unto him, In Bethlehem of Judaea: for thus it is written by the prophet,

6   And thou Bethlehem, in the land of Juda, art not the least among the princes of Juda: for out of thee shall come a Governor, that shall rule my people Israel.

7   Then Herod, when he had privily called the wise men, enquired of them diligently what time the star appeared.

8   And he sent them to Bethlehem, and said, Go and search diligently for the young child; and when ye have found him, bring me word again, that I may come and worship him also.

9   When they had heard the king, they departed; and, lo, the star, which they saw in the east, went before them, till it came and stood over where the young child was.

10   When they saw the star, they rejoiced with exceeding great joy.

11   And when they were come into the house, they saw the young child with Mary his mother, and fell down, and worshipped him: and when they had opened their treasures, they presented unto him gifts; gold, and frankincense and myrrh.

12   And being warned of God in a dream that they should not return to Herod, they departed into their own country another way.

DAVID, GERARD
Adoration of the Magi
Private Collection

THE PRESENTATION OF CHRIST IN THE TEMPLE

Luke 2

22 And when the days of her purification according to the law of Moses were accomplished, they brought him to Jerusalem, to present him to the Lord;

23 (As it is written in the law of the Lord, Every male that openeth the womb shall be called holy to the Lord;)

24 And to offer a sacrifice according to that which is said in the law of the Lord, A pair of turtledoves, or two young pigeons.

25 And, behold, there was a man in Jerusalem, whose name was Simeon; and the same man was just and devout, waiting for the consolation of Israel: and the Holy Ghost was upon him.

26 And it was revealed unto him by the Holy Ghost, that he should not see death, before he had seen the Lord's Christ.

27 And he came by the Spirit into the temple: and when the parents brought in the child Jesus, to do for him after the custom of the law,

28 Then took he him up in his arms, and blessed God, and said,

29 Lord, now lettest thou thy servant depart in peace, according to thy word:

30 For mine eyes have seen thy salvation,

31 Which thou hast prepared before the face of all people;

32 A light to lighten the Gentiles, and the glory of thy people Israel.

33 And Joseph and his mother marvelled at those things which were spoken of him.

LOTTO, LORENZO
The Presentation of Christ in the Temple
c.1556
Pinacoteca, Palazzo Apostolico, Loreto, Italy

FLIGHT INTO EGYPT
Matthew 2

13 And when they were departed, behold, the
angel of the Lord appeareth to Joseph in a dream,
saying, Arise, and take the young child and his
mother, and flee into Egypt, and be thou there until
I bring thee word: for Herod will seek the young
child to destroy him.

14 When he arose, he took the young child
and his mother by night, and departed into Egypt:

15 And was there until the death of Herod:
that it might be fulfilled which was spoken of the
Lord by the prophet, saying, Out of Egypt have
I called my son.

HESDIN, JACQUEMART DE
The Flight into Egypt
(illuminated ms.)
Bibliothèque Royale de Belgique, Brussels, Belgium

THE MASSACRE OF THE INNOCENTS

Matthew 2

16 Then Herod, when he saw that he was mocked of the wise men, was exceeding wroth, and sent forth, and slew all the children that were in Bethlehem, and in all the coasts thereof, from two years old and under, according to the time which he had diligently enquired of the wise men.

17 Then was fulfilled that which was spoken by Jeremiah the prophet, saying,

18 In Rama was there a voice heard, lamentation, and weeping, and great mourning, Rachel weeping for her children, and would not be comforted, because they are not.

19 But when Herod was dead, behold, an angel of the Lord appeareth in a dream to Joseph in Egypt,

20 Saying, Arise, and take the young child and his mother, and go into the land of Israel: for they are dead which sought the young child's life.

21 And he arose, and took the young child and his mother, and came into the land of Israel.

COGNIET, LEON
Scene of the Massacre of the Innocents
1824 (oil on canvas)
Musée des Beaux-Arts, Rennes, France

Twelve-year Old Jesus in the Temple

Luke 2

41 Now his parents went to Jerusalem every year at the feast of the passover.

42 And when he was twelve years old, they went up to Jerusalem after the custom of the feast.

43 And when they had fulfilled the days, as they returned, the child Jesus tarried behind in Jerusalem; and Joseph and his mother knew not of it.

44 But they, supposing him to have been in the company, went a day's journey; and they sought him among their kinsfolk and acquaintance.

45 And when they found him not, they turned back again to Jerusalem, seeking him.

46 And it came to pass, that after three days they found him in the temple, sitting in the midst of the doctors, both hearing them, and asking them questions.

47 And all that heard him were astonished at his understanding and answers.

48 And when they saw him, they were amazed: and his mother said unto him, Son, why hast thou thus dealt with us? behold, thy father and I have sought thee sorrowing.

49 And he said unto them, How is it that ye sought me? wist ye not that I must be about my Father's business?

50 And they understood not the saying which he spake unto them.

MENZEL, ADOLPHE VON
Twelve-year Old Jesus in the Temple
1851 (pastel and gouache on paper)
Hamburg Kunsthalle, Hamburg, Germany

St. John the Baptist
Luke 3

1   Now in the fifteenth year of the reign of Tiberius Caesar, Pontius Pilate being governor of Judaea, and Herod being tetrarch of Galilee, and his brother Philip tetrarch of Ituraea and of the region of Trachonitis, and Lysanias the tetrarch of Abilene,

2   Annas and Caiaphas being the high priests, the word of God came unto John the son of Zacharias in the wilderness.

3   And he came into all the country about Jordan, preaching the baptism of repentance for the remission of sins;

4   As it is written in the book of the words of Esaias the prophet, saying, The voice of one crying in the wilderness, Prepare ye the way of the Lord, make his paths straight.

5   Every valley shall be filled, and every mountain and hill shall be brought low; and the crooked shall be made straight, and the rough ways shall be made smooth;

6   And all flesh shall see the salvation of God.

7   Then said he to the multitude that came forth to be baptized of him, O generation of vipers, who hath warned you to flee from the wrath to come?

8   Bring forth therefore fruits worthy of repentance, and begin not to say within yourselves, We have Abraham to our father: for I say unto you, That God is able of these stones to raise up children unto Abraham.

9   And now also the axe is laid unto the root of the trees: every tree therefore which bringeth not forth good fruit is hewn down, and cast into the fire.

PALMA, JACOPO (IL VECCHIO)
St. John the Baptist
(oil on panel)
York Museums Trust (York Art Gallery), UK

THE BAPTISM OF CHRIST
Mark 1

4   John did baptize in the wilderness, and preach the baptism of repentance for the remission of sins.

5   And there went out unto him all the land of Judaea, and they of Jerusalem, and were all baptized of him in the river of Jordan, confessing their sins.

6   And John was clothed with camel's hair, and with a girdle of a skin about his loins; and he did eat locusts and wild honey;

7   And preached, saying, There cometh one mightier than I after me, the latchet of whose shoes I am not worthy to stoop down and unloose.

8   I indeed have baptized you with water: but he shall baptize you with the Holy Ghost.

9   And it came to pass in those days, that Jesus came from Nazareth of Galilee, and was baptized of John in Jordan.

10   And straightway coming up out of the water, he saw the heavens opened, and the Spirit like a dove descending upon him:

11   And there came a voice from heaven, saying, Thou art my beloved Son, in whom I am well pleased.

VERROCCHIO, ANDREA & VINCI, LEONARDO DA
The Baptism of Christ by John the Baptist
c.1475 (oil on panel)
Galleria degli Uffizi, Florence, Italy

CHRIST IN THE WILDERNESS
Luke 4

1   And Jesus being full of the Holy Ghost returned from Jordan, and was led by the Spirit into the wilderness,

2   Being forty days tempted of the devil. And in those days he did eat nothing: and when they were ended, he afterward hungered.

3   And the devil said unto him, If thou be the Son of God, command this stone that it be made bread.

4   And Jesus answered him, saying, It is written, That man shall not live by bread alone, but by every word of God.

KRAMSKOY, IVAN NIKOLAEVICH
Christ in the Wilderness
1873 (oil on canvas)
Tretyakov Gallery, Moscow, Russia

THE TEMPTATION OF CHRIST

Matthew 4

5   Then the devil taketh him up into the holy city, and setteth him on a pinnacle of the temple,

6   And saith unto him, If thou be the Son of God, cast thyself down: for it is written, He shall give his angels charge concerning thee: and in their hands they shall bear thee up, lest at any time thou dash thy foot against a stone.

7   Jesus said unto him, It is written again, Thou shalt not tempt the Lord thy God.

8   Again, the devil taketh him up into an exceeding high mountain, and sheweth him all the kingdoms of the world, and the glory of them;

9   And saith unto him, All these things will I give thee, if thou wilt fall down and worship me.

10   Then saith Jesus unto him, Get thee hence, Satan: for it is written, Thou shalt worship the Lord thy God, and him only shalt thou serve.

11   Then the devil leaveth him, and, behold, angels came and ministered unto him.

SCHEFFER, ARY
The Temptation of Christ
1854 (oil on canvas)
National Gallery of Victoria, Melbourne, Australia

CHRIST CALLING ST. PETER AND ST. ANDREW

Luke 5

1 And it came to pass, that, as the people pressed upon him to hear the word of God, he stood by the lake of Gennesaret,

2 And saw two ships standing by the lake: but the fishermen were gone out of them, and were washing their nets.

3 And he entered into one of the ships, which was Simon's, and prayed him that he would thrust out a little from the land. And he sat down, and taught the people out of the ship.

4 Now when he had left speaking, he said unto Simon, Launch out into the deep, and let down your nets for a draught.

5 And Simon answering said unto him, Master, we have toiled all the night, and have taken nothing: nevertheless at thy word I will let down the net.

6 And when they had this done, they inclosed a great multitude of fishes: and their net brake.

7 And they beckoned unto their partners, which were in the other ship, that they should come and help them. And they came, and filled both the ships, so that they began to sink.

8 When Simon Peter saw it, he fell down at Jesus' knees, saying, Depart from me; for I am a sinful man, O Lord.

9 For he was astonished, and all that were with him, at the draught of the fishes which they had taken:

10 And so was also James, and John, the sons of Zebedee, which were partners with Simon. And Jesus said unto Simon, Fear not; from henceforth thou shalt catch men.

11 And when they had brought their ships to land, they forsook all, and followed him.

TITO, DIEGO QUISPE
Christ calling St. Peter and St. Andrew
from a series of Signs of the Zodiac, 1681 (oil on canvas)
Cuzco Cathedral, Cuzco, Peru

CHRIST CALLING THE APOSTLES JAMES AND JOHN

Mark 1

19 And when he had gone a little farther thence, he saw James the son of Zebedee, and John his brother, who also were in the ship mending their nets.

20 And straightway he called them: and they left their father Zebedee in the ship with the hired servants, and went after him.

21 And they went into Capernaum; and straightway on the sabbath day he entered into the synagogue, and taught.

22 And they were astonished at his doctrine: for he taught them as one that had authority, and not as the scribes.

ARMITAGE, EDWARD A.
Christ Calling the Apostles James and John
1869
Sheffield Galleries and Museums Trust, UK

Healing a Leper
Mark 1

40 And there came a leper to him, beseeching him, and kneeling down to him, and saying unto him, If thou wilt, thou canst make me clean.

41 And Jesus, moved with compassion, put forth his hand, and touched him, and saith unto him, I will; be thou clean.

42 And as soon as he had spoken, immediately the leprosy departed from him, and he was cleansed.

43 And he straitly charged him, and forthwith sent him away;

44 And saith unto him, See thou say nothing to any man: but go thy way, shew thyself to the priest, and offer for thy cleansing those things which Moses commanded, for a testimony unto them.

45 But he went out, and began to publish it much, and to blaze abroad the matter, insomuch that Jesus could no more openly enter into the city, but was without in desert places: and they came to him from every quarter.

BYZANTINE SCHOOL (12TH CENTURY)
Jesus Healing a Leper
(mosaic)
Duomo, Monreale, Sicily, Italy

THE PARABLE OF THE SOWER

Mark 4

1   And he began again to teach by the sea side: and there was gathered unto him a great multitude, so that he entered into a ship, and sat in the sea; and the whole multitude was by the sea on the land.

2   And he taught them many things by parables, and said unto them in his doctrine,

3   Hearken; Behold, there went out a sower to sow:

4   And it came to pass, as he sowed, some fell by the way side, and the fowls of the air came and devoured it up.

5   And some fell on stony ground, where it had not much earth; and immediately it sprang up, because it had no depth of earth:

6   But when the sun was up, it was scorched; and because it had no root, it withered away.

7   And some fell among thorns, and the thorns grew up, and choked it, and it yielded no fruit.

8   And other fell on good ground, and did yield fruit that sprang up and increased; and brought forth, some thirty, and some sixty, and some an hundred.

9   And he said unto them, He that hath ears to hear, let him hear.

GRIMER, ABEL
The Parable of the Sower (April or September)
(oil on panel)
The Bowes Museum, Barnard Castle, County Durham, UK

THE SERMON ON THE MOUNT
Matthew 5

1   And seeing the multitudes, he went up into a mountain: and when he was set, his disciples came unto him:

2   And he opened his mouth, and taught them, saying,

3   Blessed are the poor in spirit: for theirs is the kingdom of heaven.

4   Blessed are they that mourn: for they shall be comforted.

5   Blessed are the meek: for they shall inherit the earth.

6   Blessed are they which do hunger and thirst after righteousness: for they shall be filled.

7   Blessed are the merciful: for they shall obtain mercy.

8   Blessed are the pure in heart: for they shall see God.

9   Blessed are the peacemakers: for they shall be called the children of God.

10   Blessed are they which are persecuted for righteousness' sake: for theirs is the kingdom of heaven.

11   Blessed are ye, when men shall revile you, and persecute you, and shall say all manner of evil against you falsely, for my sake.

12   Rejoice, and be exceeding glad: for great is your reward in heaven: for so persecuted they the prophets which were before you.

Jesus and the Centurion

Matthew 8

5 And when Jesus was entered into Capernaum, there came unto him a centurion, beseeching him,

6 And saying, Lord, my servant lieth at home sick of the palsy, grievously tormented.

7 And Jesus saith unto him, I will come and heal him.

8 The centurion answered and said, Lord, I am not worthy that thou shouldest come under my roof: but speak the word only, and my servant shall be healed.

9 For I am a man under authority, having soldiers under me: and I say to this man, Go, and he goeth; and to another, Come, and he cometh; and to my servant, Do this, and he doeth it.

10 When Jesus heard it, he marvelled, and said to them that followed, Verily I say unto you, I have not found so great faith, no, not in Israel.

11 And I say unto you, That many shall come from the east and west, and shall sit down with Abraham, and Isaac, and Jacob, in the kingdom of heaven.

12 But the children of the kingdom shall be cast out into outer darkness: there shall be weeping and gnashing of teeth.

13 And Jesus said unto the centurion, Go thy way; and as thou hast believed, so be it done unto thee. And his servant was healed in the selfsame hour.

VERONESE, (PAOLO CALIARI)
Jesus and the Centurion
(oil on canvas)
Prado, Madrid, Spain

HEALING OF THE PARALYTIC

Matthew 9

1   And he entered into a ship, and passed over, and came into his own city.

2   And, behold, they brought to him a man sick of the palsy, lying on a bed: and Jesus seeing their faith said unto the sick of the palsy; Son, be of good cheer; thy sins be forgiven thee.

3   And, behold, certain of the scribes said within themselves, This man blasphemeth.

4   And Jesus knowing their thoughts said, Wherefore think ye evil in your hearts?

5   For whether is easier, to say, Thy sins be forgiven thee; or to say, Arise, and walk?

6   But that ye may know that the Son of man hath power on earth to forgive sins, (then saith he to the sick of the palsy,) Arise, take up thy bed, and go unto thine house.

7   And he arose, and departed to his house.

8   But when the multitudes saw it, they marvelled, and glorified God, which had given such power unto men.

BULGARIAN SCHOOL,
The Healing of the Paralytic
1811 (oil on panel)
Rila Monastery National Museum, Bulgaria

THE CALLING OF ST. MATTHEW
Matthew 9

9 And as Jesus passed forth from thence, he saw a man, named Matthew, sitting at the receipt of custom: and he saith unto him, Follow me. And he arose, and followed him.

10 And it came to pass, as Jesus sat at meat in the house, behold, many publicans and sinners came and sat down with him and his disciples.

11 And when the Pharisees saw it, they said unto his disciples, Why eateth your Master with publicans and sinners?

12 But when Jesus heard that, he said unto them, They that be whole need not a physician, but they that are sick.

13 But go ye and learn what that meaneth, I will have mercy, and not sacrifice: for I am not come to call the righteous, but sinners to repentance.

14 Then came to him the disciples of John, saying, Why do we and the Pharisees fast oft, but thy disciples fast not?

15 And Jesus said unto them, Can the children of the bridechamber mourn, as long as the bridegroom is with them? but the days will come, when the bridegroom shall be taken from them, and then shall they fast.

16 No man putteth a piece of new cloth unto an old garment, for that which is put in to fill it up taketh from the garment, and the rent is made worse.

17 Neither do men put new wine into old bottles: else the bottles break, and the wine runneth out, and the bottles perish: but they put new wine into new bottles, and both are preserved.

CARAVAGGIO, MICHELANGELO MERISI DA
The Calling of St. Matthew
c.1598-1601 (oil on panel)
Contarelli Chapel, S. Luigi dei Francesi, Rome, Italy

The Wedding at Cana

John 2

1   And the third day there was a marriage in Cana of Galilee; and the mother of Jesus was there:

2   And both Jesus was called, and his disciples, to the marriage.

3   And when they wanted wine, the mother of Jesus saith unto him, They have no wine.

4   Jesus saith unto her, Woman, what have I to do with thee? mine hour is not yet come.

5   His mother saith unto the servants, Whatsoever he saith unto you, do it.

6   And there were set there six waterpots of stone, after the manner of the purifying of the Jews, containing two or three firkins apiece.

7   Jesus saith unto them, Fill the waterpots with water. And they filled them up to the brim.

8   And he saith unto them, Draw out now, and bear unto the governor of the feast. And they bare it.

9   When the ruler of the feast had tasted the water that was made wine, and knew not whence it was: (but the servants which drew the water knew;) the governor of the feast called the bridegroom,

10   And saith unto him, Every man at the beginning doth set forth good wine; and when men have well drunk, then that which is worse: but thou hast kept the good wine until now.

11   This beginning of miracles did Jesus in Cana of Galilee, and manifested forth his glory; and his disciples believed on him.

MURILLO, BARTOLOME ESTEBAN
The Marriage Feast at Cana
c.1665-75
The Barber Institute of Fine Arts, University of Birmingham

CHRIST INSTRUCTING NICODEMUS

John 3

1   There was a man of the Pharisees, named Nicodemus, a ruler of the Jews:

2   The same came to Jesus by night, and said unto him, Rabbi, we know that thou art a teacher come from God: for no man can do these miracles that thou doest, except God be with him.

3   Jesus answered and said unto him, Verily, verily, I say unto thee, Except a man be born again, he cannot see the kingdom of God.

4   Nicodemus saith unto him, How can a man be born when he is old? can he enter the second time into his mother's womb, and be born?

5   Jesus answered, Verily, verily, I say unto thee, Except a man be born of water and of the Spirit, he cannot enter into the kingdom of God.

6   That which is born of the flesh is flesh; and that which is born of the Spirit is spirit.

7   Marvel not that I said unto thee, Ye must be born again.

8   The wind bloweth where it listeth, and thou hearest the sound thereof, but canst not tell whence it cometh, and whither it goeth: so is every one that is born of the Spirit.

9   Nicodemus answered and said unto him, How can these things be?

10   Jesus answered and said unto him, Art thou a master of Israel, and knowest not these things?

11   Verily, verily, I say unto thee, We speak that we do know, and testify that we have seen; and ye receive not our witness.

12   If I have told you earthly things, and ye believe not, how shall ye believe, if I tell you of heavenly things?

13   And no man hath ascended up to heaven, but he that came down from heaven, even the Son of man which is in heaven.

14   And as Moses lifted up the serpent in the wilderness, even so must the Son of man be lifted up:

15   That whosoever believeth in him should not perish, but have eternal life.

16   For God so loved the world, that he gave his only begotten Son, that whosoever believeth in him should not perish, but have everlasting life.

JORDAENS, JACOB
Christ Instructing Nicodemus
(oil on canvas)
Musée des Beaux-Arts, Tournai, Belgium

CHRIST IN THE HOUSE OF SIMON THE PHARISEE

Luke 7

36 And one of the Pharisees desired him that he would eat with him. And he went into the Pharisee's house, and sat down to meat.

37 And, behold, a woman in the city, which was a sinner, when she knew that Jesus sat at meat in the Pharisee's house, brought an alabaster box of ointment,

38 And stood at his feet behind him weeping, and began to wash his feet with tears, and did wipe them with the hairs of her head, and kissed his feet, and anointed them with the ointment.

39 Now when the Pharisee which had bidden him saw it, he spake within himself, saying, This man, if he were a prophet, would have known who and what manner of woman this is that toucheth him: for she is a sinner.

40 And Jesus answering said unto him, Simon, I have somewhat to say unto thee. And he saith, Master, say on.

41 There was a certain creditor which had two debtors: the one owed five hundred pence, and the other fifty.

42 And when they had nothing to pay, he frankly forgave them both. Tell me therefore, which of them will love him most?

43 Simon answered and said, I suppose that he, to whom he forgave most. And he said unto him, Thou hast rightly judged.

44 And he turned to the woman, and said unto Simon, Seest thou this woman? I entered into thine house, thou gavest me no water for my feet: but she hath washed my feet with tears, and wiped them with the hairs of her head.

45 Thou gavest me no kiss: but this woman since the time I came in hath not ceased to kiss my feet.

46 My head with oil thou didst not anoint: but this woman hath anointed my feet with ointment.

47 Wherefore I say unto thee, Her sins, which are many, are forgiven; for she loved much: but to whom little is forgiven, the same loveth little.

48 And he said unto her, Thy sins are forgiven.

49 And they that sat at meat with him began to say within themselves, Who is this that forgiveth sins also?

50 And he said to the woman, Thy faith hath saved thee; go in peace.

CHRIST AND THE WOMAN OF SAMARIA

John 4

3   He left Judaea, and departed again into Galilee.

4   And he must needs go through Samaria.

5   Then cometh he to a city of Samaria, which is called Sychar, near to the parcel of ground that Jacob gave to his son Joseph.

6   Now Jacob's well was there. Jesus therefore, being wearied with his journey, sat thus on the well: and it was about the sixth hour.

7   There cometh a woman of Samaria to draw water: Jesus saith unto her, Give me to drink.

8   (For his disciples were gone away unto the city to buy meat.)

9   Then saith the woman of Samaria unto him, How is it that thou, being a Jew, askest drink of me, which am a woman of Samaria? for the Jews have no dealings with the Samaritans.

10   Jesus answered and said unto her, If thou knewest the gift of God, and who it is that saith to thee, Give me to drink; thou wouldest have asked of him, and he would have given thee living water.

11   The woman saith unto him, Sir, thou hast nothing to draw with, and the well is deep: from whence then hast thou that living water?

12   Art thou greater than our father Jacob, which gave us the well, and drank thereof himself, and his children, and his cattle?

13   Jesus answered and said unto her, Whosoever drinketh of this water shall thirst again:

14   But whosoever drinketh of the water that I shall give him shall never thirst; but the water that I shall give him shall be in him a well of water springing up into everlasting life.

TINTORETTO, DOMENICO ROBUSTI
Christ and the Woman of Samaria
(oil on canvas)
© The Barnes Foundation, Merion, Pennsylvania, USA

THE POOL OF BETHESDA

John 5

1   After this there was a feast of the Jews; and Jesus went up to Jerusalem.

2   Now there is at Jerusalem by the sheep market a pool, which is called in the Hebrew tongue Bethesda, having five porches.

3   In these lay a great multitude of impotent folk, of blind, halt, withered, waiting for the moving of the water.

4   For an angel went down at a certain season into the pool, and troubled the water: whosoever then first after the troubling of the water stepped in was made whole of whatsoever disease he had.

5   And a certain man was there, which had an infirmity thirty and eight years.

6   When Jesus saw him lie, and knew that he had been now a long time in that case, he saith unto him, Wilt thou be made whole?

7   The impotent man answered him, Sir, I have no man, when the water is troubled, to put me into the pool: but while I am coming, another steppeth down before me.

8   Jesus saith unto him, Rise, take up thy bed, and walk.

9   And immediately the man was made whole, and took up his bed, and walked: and on the same day was the sabbath.

DELEN, DIRCK VAN
The Pool of Bethesda
1645 (oil on panel)
Private Collection

Salome Dancing at the Feast of Herod

Matthew 14

1   At that time Herod the tetrarch heard of the fame of Jesus,

2   And said unto his servants, This is John the Baptist; he is risen from the dead; and therefore mighty works do shew forth themselves in him.

3   For Herod had laid hold on John, and bound him, and put him in prison for Herodias' sake, his brother Philip's wife.

4   For John said unto him, It is not lawful for thee to have her.

5   And when he would have put him to death, he feared the multitude, because they counted him as a prophet.

6   But when Herod's birthday was kept, the daughter of Herodias danced before them, and pleased Herod.

7   Whereupon he promised with an oath to give her whatsoever she would ask.

8   And she, being before instructed of her mother, said, Give me here John Baptist's head in a charger.

9   And the king was sorry: nevertheless for the oath's sake, and them which sat with him at meat, he commanded it to be given her.

10   And he sent, and beheaded John in the prison.

11   And his head was brought in a charger, and given to the damsel: and she brought it to her mother.

12   And his disciples came, and took up the body, and buried it, and went and told Jesus.

LIPPI, FRA FILIPPO
Salome Dancing at the Feast of Herod
detail of the fresco cycle of the Lives of the SS. Stephen and John the Baptist, 1452-64 (fresco)
Duomo, Prato, Italy

Cure of a Woman Who Bleeds and The Raising of Jairus' Daughter

Mark 5

21 And when Jesus was passed over again by ship unto the other side, much people gathered unto him: and he was nigh unto the sea.

22 And, behold, there cometh one of the rulers of the synagogue, Jairus by name; and when he saw him, he fell at his feet,

23 And besought him greatly, saying, My little daughter lieth at the point of death: I pray thee, come and lay thy hands on her, that she may be healed; and she shall live.

24 And Jesus went with him; and much people followed him, and thronged him.

25 And a certain woman, which had an issue of blood twelve years,

26 And had suffered many things of many physicians, and had spent all that she had, and was nothing bettered, but rather grew worse,

27 When she had heard of Jesus, came in the press behind, and touched his garment.

28 For she said, If I may touch but his clothes, I shall be whole.

29 And straightway the fountain of her blood was dried up; and she felt in her body that she was healed of that plague.

30 And Jesus, immediately knowing in himself that virtue had gone out of him, turned him about in the press, and said, Who touched my clothes?

31 And his disciples said unto him, Thou seest the multitude thronging thee, and sayest thou, Who touched me?

32 And he looked round about to see her that had done this thing.

33 But the woman fearing and trembling, knowing what was done in her, came and fell down before him, and told him all the truth.

34 And he said unto her, Daughter, thy faith hath made thee whole; go in peace, and be whole of thy plague.

35 While he yet spake, there came from the ruler of the synagogue's house certain which said, Thy daughter is dead: why troublest thou the Master any further?

36 As soon as Jesus heard the word that was spoken, he saith unto the ruler of the synagogue, Be not afraid, only believe.

37 And he suffered no man to follow him, save Peter, and James, and John the brother of James.

38 And he cometh to the house of the ruler of the synagogue, and seeth the tumult, and them that wept and wailed greatly.

39 And when he was come in, he saith unto them, Why make ye this ado, and weep? the damsel is not dead, but sleepeth.

40 And they laughed him to scorn. But when he had put them all out, he taketh the father and the mother of the damsel, and them that were with him, and entereth in where the damsel was lying.

41 And he took the damsel by the hand, and said unto her, Talitha cumi; which is, being interpreted, Damsel, I say unto thee, arise.

42 And straightway the damsel arose, and walked; for she was of the age of twelve years. And they were astonished with a great astonishment.

43 And he charged them straitly that no man should know it; and commanded that something should be given her to eat.

PALEO-CHRISTIAN
Jesus Cures the Woman Who Bleeds
late 3rd century (fresco)
Cimitero dei SS. Marcellino e Pietro, Rome, Italy

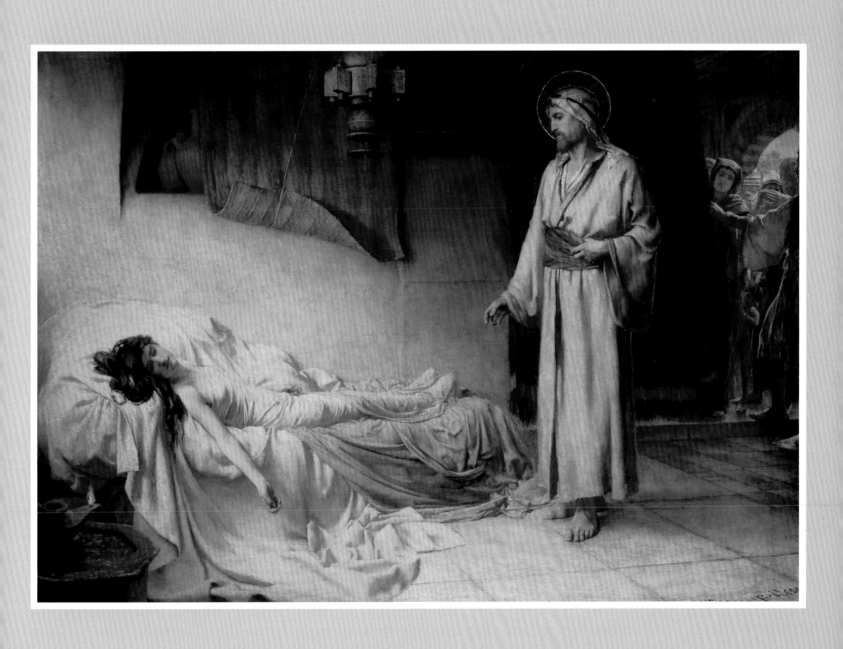

JACOMB-HOOD, GEORGE PERCY
The Raising of Jairus' Daughter
Guildhall Art Gallery, Corporation of London, UK

THE FEEDING OF THE FIVE THOUSAND

Luke 9

12 And when the day began to wear away, then came the twelve, and said unto him, Send the multitude away, that they may go into the towns and country round about, and lodge, and get victuals: for we are here in a desert place.

13 But he said unto them, Give ye them to eat. And they said, We have no more but five loaves and two fishes; except we should go and buy meat for all this people.

14 For they were about five thousand men. And he said to his disciples, Make them sit down by fifties in a company.

15 And they did so, and made them all sit down.

16 Then he took the five loaves and the two fishes, and looking up to heaven, he blessed them, and brake, and gave to the disciples to set before the multitude.

17 And they did eat, and were all filled: and there was taken up of fragments that remained to them twelve baskets.

PATINIR, JOACHIM
The Feeding of the Five Thousand
(oil on panel)
Monasterio de El Escorial, Spain

CHRIST IN THE STORM ON THE SEA OF GALILEE

Matthew 14

22 And straightway Jesus constrained his disciples to get into a ship, and to go before him unto the other side, while he sent the multitudes away.

23 And when he had sent the multitudes away, he went up into a mountain apart to pray: and when the evening was come, he was there alone.

24 But the ship was now in the midst of the sea, tossed with waves: for the wind was contrary.

25 And in the fourth watch of the night Jesus went unto them, walking on the sea.

26 And when the disciples saw him walking on the sea, they were troubled, saying, It is a spirit; and they cried out for fear.

27 But straightway Jesus spake unto them, saying, Be of good cheer; it is I; be not afraid.

28 And Peter answered him and said, Lord, if it be thou, bid me come unto thee on the water.

29 And he said, Come. And when Peter was come down out of the ship, he walked on the water, to go to Jesus.

30 But when he saw the wind boisterous, he was afraid; and beginning to sink, he cried, saying, Lord, save me.

31 And immediately Jesus stretched forth his hand, and caught him, and said unto him, O thou of little faith, wherefore didst thou doubt?

32 And when they were come into the ship, the wind ceased.

33 Then they that were in the ship came and worshipped him, saying, Of a truth thou art the Son of God.

BACKHUYSEN, LUDOLF
Christ in the Storm on the Sea of Galilee
1695 (oil on canvas)
Noortman, Maastricht, Netherlands

THE TRANSFIGURATION
Mark 9

2   And after six days Jesus taketh with him Peter, and James, and John, and leadeth them up into an high mountain apart by themselves: and he was transfigured before them.

3   And his raiment became shining, exceeding white as snow; so as no fuller on earth can white them.

4   And there appeared unto them Elias with Moses: and they were talking with Jesus.

5   And Peter answered and said to Jesus, Master, it is good for us to be here: and let us make three tabernacles; one for thee, and one for Moses, and one for Elias.

6   For he wist not what to say; for they were sore afraid.

7   And there was a cloud that overshadowed them: and a voice came out of the cloud, saying, This is my beloved Son: hear him.

8   And suddenly, when they had looked round about, they saw no man any more, save Jesus only with themselves.

9   And as they came down from the mountain, he charged them that they should tell no man what things they had seen, till the Son of man were risen from the dead.

CARRACCI, LODOVICO
The Transfiguration
1594-95 (oil on canvas)
Pinacoteca Nazionale, Bologna, Italy

THE GOOD SAMARITAN
Luke 10

25 And, behold, a certain lawyer stood up, and tempted him, saying, Master, what shall I do to inherit eternal life?

26 He said unto him, What is written in the law? how readest thou?

27 And he answering said, Thou shalt love the Lord thy God with all thy heart, and with all thy soul, and with all thy strength, and with all thy mind; and thy neighbour as thyself.

28 And he said unto him, Thou hast answered right: this do, and thou shalt live.

29 But he, willing to justify himself, said unto Jesus, And who is my neighbour?

30 And Jesus answering said, A certain man went down from Jerusalem to Jericho, and fell among thieves, which stripped him of his raiment, and wounded him, and departed, leaving him half dead.

31 And by chance there came down a certain priest that way: and when he saw him, he passed by on the other side.

32 And likewise a Levite, when he was at the place, came and looked on him, and passed by on the other side.

33 But a certain Samaritan, as he journeyed, came where he was: and when he saw him, he had compassion on him,

34 And went to him, and bound up his wounds, pouring in oil and wine, and set him on his own beast, and brought him to an inn, and took care of him.

35 And on the morrow when he departed, he took out two pence, and gave them to the host, and said unto him, Take care of him; and whatsoever thou spendest more, when I come again, I will repay thee.

36 Which now of these three, thinkest thou, was neighbour unto him that fell among the thieves?

37 And he said, He that shewed mercy on him. Then said Jesus unto him, Go, and do thou likewise.

CORNELISZ. VAN HAARLEM, CORNELIS
The Good Samaritan
1627 (panel)
Johnny van Haeften Gallery, London, UK

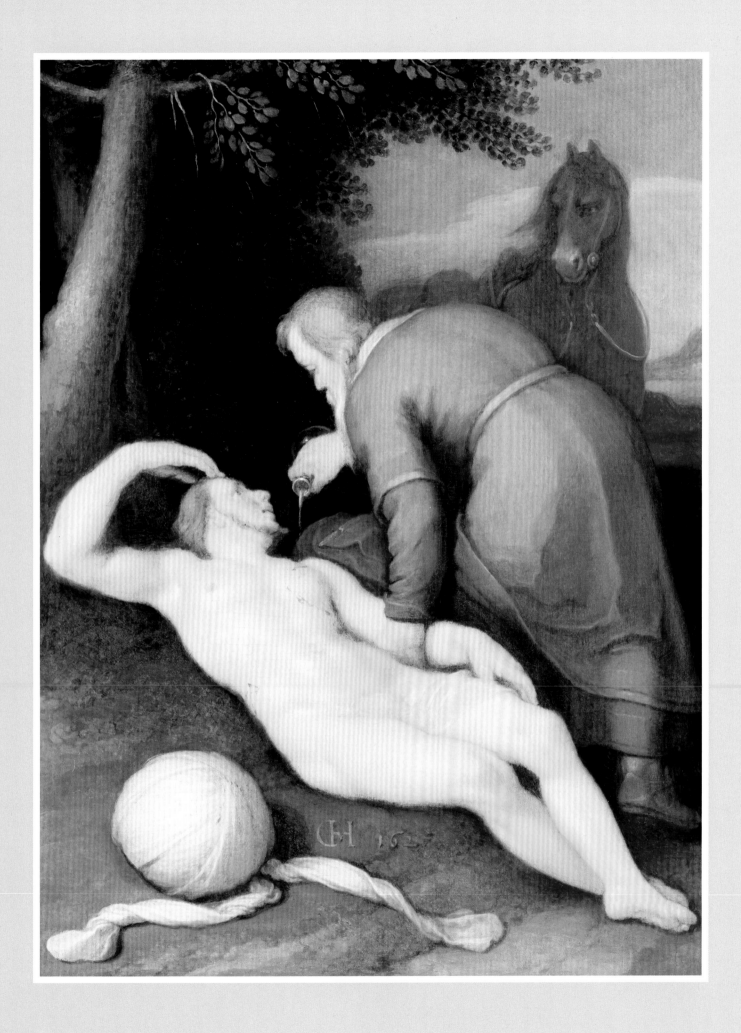

CHRIST IN THE HOUSE OF MARTHA AND MARY

Luke 10

38 Now it came to pass, as they went, that he entered into a certain village: and a certain woman named Martha received him into her house.

39 And she had a sister called Mary, which also sat at Jesus' feet, and heard his word.

40 But Martha was cumbered about much serving, and came to him, and said, Lord, dost thou not care that my sister hath left me to serve alone? bid her therefore that she help me.

41 And Jesus answered and said unto her, Martha, Martha, thou art careful and troubled about many things:

42 But one thing is needful: and Mary hath chosen that good part, which shall not be taken away from her.

150
VERMEER, JAN
Christ in the House of Martha and Mary
c.1654-56
National Gallery of Scotland, Edinburgh, Scotland

THE WOMAN TAKEN IN ADULTERY

John 8

1 Jesus went unto the mount of Olives.

2 And early in the morning he came again into the temple, and all the people came unto him; and he sat down, and taught them.

3 And the scribes and Pharisees brought unto him a woman taken in adultery; and when they had set her in the midst,

4 They say unto him, Master, this woman was taken in adultery, in the very act.

5 Now Moses in the law commanded us, that such should be stoned: but what sayest thou?

6 This they said, tempting him, that they might have to accuse him. But Jesus stooped down, and with his finger wrote on the ground, as though he heard them not.

7 So when they continued asking him, he lifted up himself, and said unto them, He that is without sin among you, let him first cast a stone at her.

8 And again he stooped down, and wrote on the ground.

9 And they which heard it, being convicted by their own conscience, went out one by one, beginning at the eldest, even unto the last: and Jesus was left alone, and the woman standing in the midst.

10 When Jesus had lifted up himself, and saw none but the woman, he said unto her, Woman, where are those thine accusers? hath no man condemned thee?

11 She said, No man, Lord. And Jesus said unto her, Neither do I condemn thee: go, and sin no more.

POUSSIN, NICOLAS
The Woman Taken in Adultery
1653 (oil on canvas)
Louvre, Paris, France

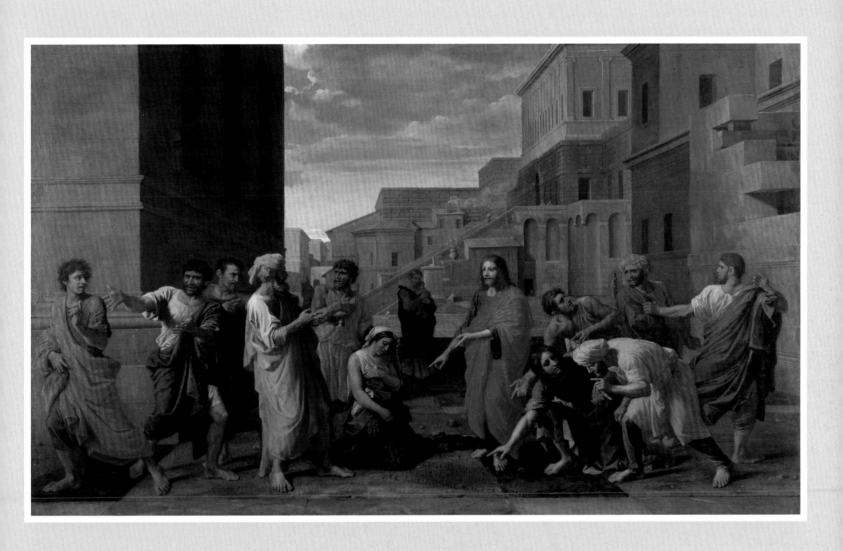

THE GOOD SHEPHERD
John 10

7 Then said Jesus unto them again, Verily, verily, I say unto you, I am the door of the sheep.

8 All that ever came before me are thieves and robbers: but the sheep did not hear them.

9 I am the door: by me if any man enter in, he shall be saved, and shall go in and out, and find pasture.

10 The thief cometh not, but for to steal, and to kill, and to destroy: I am come that they might have life, and that they might have it more abundantly.

11 I am the good shepherd: the good shepherd giveth his life for the sheep.

12 But he that is an hireling, and not the shepherd, whose own the sheep are not, seeth the wolf coming, and leaveth the sheep, and fleeth: and the wolf catcheth them, and scattereth the sheep.

13 The hireling fleeth, because he is an hireling, and careth not for the sheep.

14 I am the good shepherd, and know my sheep, and am known of mine.

15 As the Father knoweth me, even so know I the Father: and I lay down my life for the sheep.

16 And other sheep I have, which are not of this fold: them also I must bring, and they shall hear my voice; and there shall be one fold, and one shepherd.

17 Therefore doth my Father love me, because I lay down my life, that I might take it again.

18 No man taketh it from me, but I lay it down of myself. I have power to lay it down, and I have power to take it again. This commandment have I received of my Father.

CHAMPAIGNE, PHILIPPE DE
The Good Shepherd
(oil on canvas)
Musée des Beaux-Arts, Lille, France

THE RAISING OF LAZARUS
John 11

30 Now Jesus was not yet come into the town, but was in that place where Martha met him.

31 The Jews then which were with her in the house, and comforted her, when they saw Mary, that she rose up hastily and went out, followed her, saying, She goeth unto the grave to weep there.

32 Then when Mary was come where Jesus was, and saw him, she fell down at his feet, saying unto him, Lord, if thou hadst been here, my brother had not died.

33 When Jesus therefore saw her weeping, and the Jews also weeping which came with her, he groaned in the spirit, and was troubled.

34 And said, Where have ye laid him? They said unto him, Lord, come and see.

35 Jesus wept.

36 Then said the Jews, Behold how he loved him!

37 And some of them said, Could not this man, which opened the eyes of the blind, have caused that even this man should not have died?

38 Jesus therefore again groaning in himself cometh to the grave. It was a cave, and a stone lay upon it.

39 Jesus said, Take ye away the stone. Martha, the sister of him that was dead, saith unto him, Lord, by this time he stinketh: for he hath been dead four days.

40 Jesus saith unto her, Said I not unto thee, that, if thou wouldest believe, thou shouldest see the glory of God?

41 Then they took away the stone from the place where the dead was laid. And Jesus lifted up his eyes, and said, Father, I thank thee that thou hast heard me.

42 And I knew that thou hearest me always: but because of the people which stand by I said it, that they may believe that thou hast sent me.

43 And when he thus had spoken, he cried with a loud voice, Lazarus, come forth.

44 And he that was dead came forth, bound hand and foot with graveclothes: and his face was bound about with a napkin. Jesus saith unto them, Loose him, and let him go.

45 Then many of the Jews which came to Mary, and had seen the things which Jesus did, believed on him.

GIOTTO DI BONDONE
The Raising of Lazarus
c.1305 (fresco) (post restoration)
Scrovegni (Arena) Chapel, Padua, Italy

JESUS GIVES THE KEYS TO ST. PETER

Matthew 16

13 When Jesus came into the coasts of Caesarea Philippi, he asked his disciples, saying, Whom do men say that I the Son of man am?

14 And they said, Some say that thou art John the Baptist: some, Elias; and others, Jeremias, or one of the prophets.

15 He saith unto them, But whom say ye that I am?

16 And Simon Peter answered and said, Thou art the Christ, the Son of the living God.

17 And Jesus answered and said unto him, Blessed art thou, Simon Barjona: for flesh and blood hath not revealed it unto thee, but my Father which is in heaven.

18 And I say also unto thee, That thou art Peter, and upon this rock I will build my church; and the gates of hell shall not prevail against it.

19 And I will give unto thee the keys of the kingdom of heaven: and whatsoever thou shalt bind on earth shall be bound in heaven: and whatsoever thou shalt loose on earth shall be loosed in heaven.

20 Then charged he his disciples that they should tell no man that he was Jesus the Christ.

INGRES, JEAN AUGUSTE DOMINIQUE
Jesus Returning the Keys to St. Peter
1820 (oil on canvas)
Musée Ingres, Montauban, France

THE PRODIGAL SON
Luke 15

11   And he said, A certain man had two sons:

12   And the younger of them said to his father, Father, give me the portion of goods that falleth to me. And he divided unto them his living.

13   And not many days after the younger son gathered all together, and took his journey into a far country, and there wasted his substance with riotous living.

14   And when he had spent all, there arose a mighty famine in that land; and he began to be in want.

15   And he went and joined himself to a citizen of that country; and he sent him into his fields to feed swine.

16   And he would fain have filled his belly with the husks that the swine did eat: and no man gave unto him.

17   And when he came to himself, he said, How many hired servants of my father's have bread enough and to spare, and I perish with hunger!

18   I will arise and go to my father, and will say unto him, Father, I have sinned against heaven, and before thee,

19   And am no more worthy to be called thy son: make me as one of thy hired servants.

20   And he arose, and came to his father. But when he was yet a great way off, his father saw him, and had compassion, and ran, and fell on his neck, and kissed him.

21   And the son said unto him, Father, I have sinned against heaven, and in thy sight, and am no more worthy to be called thy son.

22   But the father said to his servants, Bring forth the best robe, and put it on him; and put a ring on his hand, and shoes on his feet:

23   And bring hither the fatted calf, and kill it; and let us eat, and be merry:

24   For this my son was dead, and is alive again; he was lost, and is found. And they began to be merry.

GUERCINO (GIOVANNI FRANCESCO BARBIERI)
The Prodigal Son
(oil on canvas)
Galleria Borghese, Rome, Italy

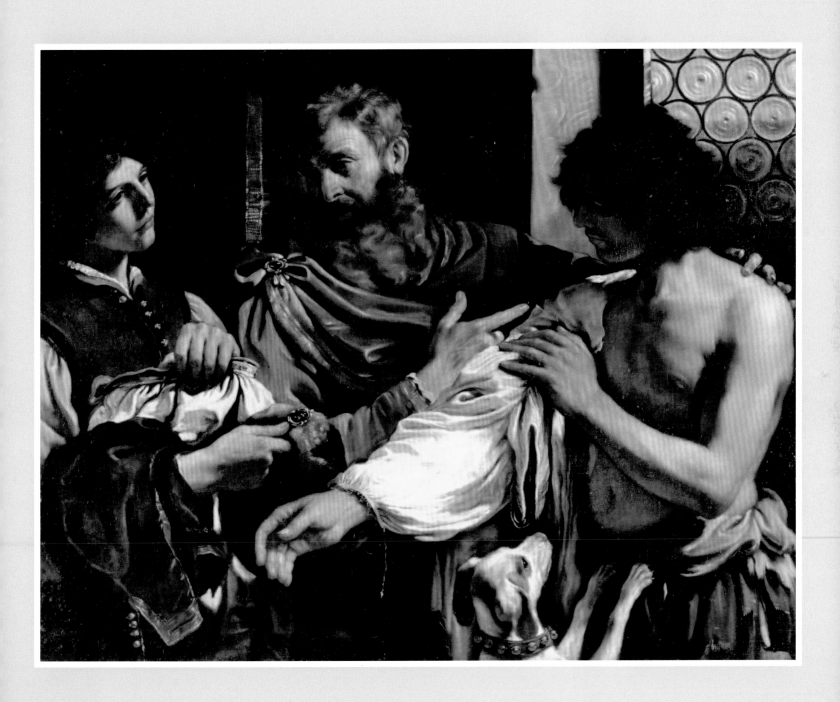

Lazarus and the Rich Man's Table

Luke 16

19 There was a certain rich man, which was clothed in purple and fine linen, and fared sumptuously every day:

20 And there was a certain beggar named Lazarus, which was laid at his gate, full of sores,

21 And desiring to be fed with the crumbs which fell from the rich man's table: moreover the dogs came and licked his sores.

22 And it came to pass, that the beggar died, and was carried by the angels into Abraham's bosom: the rich man also died, and was buried;

23 And in hell he lift up his eyes, being in torments, and seeth Abraham afar off, and Lazarus in his bosom.

24 And he cried and said, Father Abraham, have mercy on me, and send Lazarus, that he may dip the tip of his finger in water, and cool my tongue; for I am tormented in this flame.

25 But Abraham said, Son, remember that thou in thy lifetime receivedst thy good things, and likewise Lazarus evil things: but now he is comforted, and thou art tormented.

26 And beside all this, between us and you there is a great gulf fixed: so that they which would pass from hence to you cannot; neither can they pass to us, that would come from thence.

27 Then he said, I pray thee therefore, father, that thou wouldest send him to my father's house:

28 For I have five brethren; that he may testify unto them, lest they also come into this place of torment.

29 Abraham saith unto him, They have Moses and the prophets; let them hear them.

30 And he said, Nay, father Abraham: but if one went unto them from the dead, they will repent.

31 And he said unto him, If they hear not Moses and the prophets, neither will they be persuaded, though one rose from the dead.

Gerung or Gerou, Matthias
Lazarus and the Rich Man's Table
from the Mompelgarter Altarpiece (panel)
Kunsthistorisches Museum, Vienna, Austria

Es was aber ein reycher man / der kleydet sich mit purpur / ꝛc. vnd lebet
alle tag herlich wol / Es was aber ein armer mit namen Lazarus
der lag vor seiner thür voller gschwär / vnd begert sich zů settigen võ
den brosamen die von des reychen tisch fielen / Doch leckten im die
hund seine gschwär / Es begab sich aber das der arm starb / vnd
ward getragen von den engeln gottes in Abrahams schoß / d́ reych
aber starb auch / vnd ward begrabẽ / Als er nun in d́ qual sahe
abraham vnd Lazarũ / begert er eins tropfen wassers sein
zungen zů külen / deßgleychẽ
mer / ward
im versagt
ꝛc.

Luc. 16.

CHRIST HEALING THE BLIND MAN OF JERICHO
Mark 10

46 And they came to Jericho: and as he went out of Jericho with his disciples and a great number of people, blind Bartimaeus, the son of Timaeus, sat by the highway side begging.

47 And when he heard that it was Jesus of Nazareth, he began to cry out, and say, Jesus, thou son of David, have mercy on me.

48 And many charged him that he should hold his peace: but he cried the more a great deal, Thou son of David, have mercy on me.

49 And Jesus stood still, and commanded him to be called. And they call the blind man, saying unto him, Be of good comfort, rise; he calleth thee.

50 And he, casting away his garment, rose, and came to Jesus.

51 And Jesus answered and said unto him, What wilt thou that I should do unto thee? The blind man said unto him, Lord, that I might receive my sight.

52 And Jesus said unto him, Go thy way; thy faith hath made thee whole. And immediately he received his sight, and followed Jesus in the way.

POUSSIN, NICOLAS
The Blind of Jericho, or Christ Healing the Blind
1650 (oil on canvas)
Louvre, Paris, France

ENTRY OF CHRIST INTO JERUSALEM

John 12

1 Then Jesus six days before the passover came to Bethany, where Lazarus was, which had been dead, whom he raised from the dead.

2 There they made him a supper; and Martha served: but Lazarus was one of them that sat at the table with him.

3 Then took Mary a pound of ointment of spikenard, very costly, and anointed the feet of Jesus, and wiped his feet with her hair: and the house was filled with the odour of the ointment.

4 Then saith one of his disciples, Judas Iscariot, Simon's son, which should betray him,

5 Why was not this ointment sold for three hundred pence, and given to the poor?

6 This he said, not that he cared for the poor; but because he was a thief, and had the bag, and bare what was put therein.

7 Then said Jesus, Let her alone: against the day of my burying hath she kept this.

8 For the poor always ye have with you; but me ye have not always.

9 Much people of the Jews therefore knew that he was there: and they came not for Jesus' sake only, but that they might see Lazarus also, whom he had raised from the dead.

10 But the chief priests consulted that they might put Lazarus also to death;

11 Because that by reason of him many of the Jews went away, and believed on Jesus.

12 On the next day much people that were come to the feast, when they heard that Jesus was coming to Jerusalem,

13 Took branches of palm trees, and went forth to meet him, and cried, Hosanna: Blessed is the King of Israel that cometh in the name of the Lord.

14 And Jesus, when he had found a young ass, sat thereon; as it is written,

15 Fear not, daughter of Sion: behold, thy King cometh, sitting on an ass's colt.

16 These things understood not his disciples at the first: but when Jesus was glorified, then remembered they that these things were written of him, and that they had done these things unto him.

ANGELICO, FRA (GUIDO DI PIETRO) (AND WORKSHOP)
Entry of Christ into Jerusalem
detail from panel three of the Silver Treasury of Santissima Annunziata, c.1450-53 (tempera on panel)
Museo di San Marco dell'Angelico, Florence, Italy

CCE REX TVVS VENIT TIBI MANSVETVS SEDES SVP ASINA ZFILIV SVBIVGAL CACHARI .IX.

OSANNA FILIO DAVID BENEDICTVS QVI VENIT IN NOMINE DOMINI . MACTEI . XXI .

60 ÎMOLABO VOBIS VICTIMA SVP MONTEM VT OMEDATIS CARNES ZBIBATIS SANGVINE .EGECHI.XXXII.

CHRIST DRIVING THE MONEY-CHANGERS FROM THE TEMPLE

Mark 11

11 And Jesus entered into Jerusalem, and into the temple: and when he had looked round about upon all things, and now the eventide was come, he went out unto Bethany with the twelve.

12 And on the morrow, when they were come from Bethany, he was hungry:

13 And seeing a fig tree afar off having leaves, he came, if haply he might find any thing thereon: and when he came to it, he found nothing but leaves; for the time of figs was not yet.

14 And Jesus answered and said unto it, No man eat fruit of thee hereafter for ever. And his disciples heard it.

15 And they come to Jerusalem: and Jesus went into the temple, and began to cast out them that sold and bought in the temple, and overthrew the tables of the moneychangers, and the seats of them that sold doves;

16 And would not suffer that any man should carry any vessel through the temple.

17 And he taught, saying unto them, Is it not written, My house shall be called of all nations the house of prayer? but ye have made it a den of thieves.

18 And the scribes and chief priests heard it, and sought how they might destroy him: for they feared him, because all the people was astonished at his doctrine.

19 And when even was come, he went out of the city.

GAROFALO, BENVENUTO TISI DA
Christ Driving the Money-Changers from the Temple
(panel)
National Gallery of Scotland, Edinburgh, Scotland

CHRIST WASHING THE DISCIPLES' FEET
John 13

1   Now before the feast of the passover, when Jesus knew that his hour was come that he should depart out of this world unto the Father, having loved his own which were in the world, he loved them unto the end.

2   And supper being ended, the devil having now put into the heart of Judas Iscariot, Simon's son, to betray him;

3   Jesus knowing that the Father had given all things into his hands, and that he was come from God, and went to God;

4   He riseth from supper, and laid aside his garments; and took a towel, and girded himself.

5   After that he poureth water into a bason, and began to wash the disciples' feet, and to wipe them with the towel wherewith he was girded.

6   Then cometh he to Simon Peter: and Peter saith unto him, Lord, dost thou wash my feet?

7   Jesus answered and said unto him, What I do thou knowest not now; but thou shalt know hereafter.

8   Peter saith unto him, Thou shalt never wash my feet. Jesus answered him, If I wash thee not, thou hast no part with me.

9   Simon Peter saith unto him, Lord, not my feet only, but also my hands and my head.

10   Jesus saith to him, He that is washed needeth not save to wash his feet, but is clean every whit: and ye are clean, but not all.

11   For he knew who should betray him; therefore said he, Ye are not all clean.

WTEWAEL, PETER
Christ Washing the Disciples' Feet
1623 (oil on panel)
Musée des Beaux-Arts, Arras, France

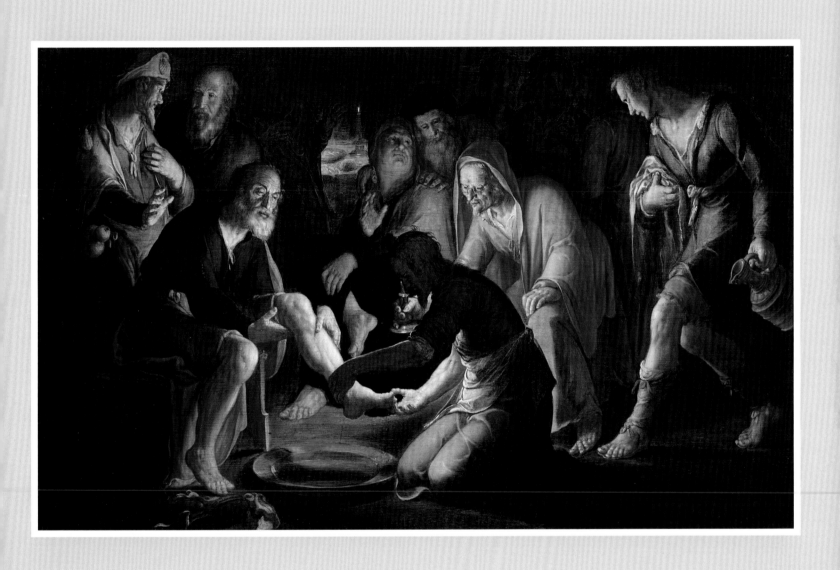

THE LAST SUPPER
Luke 22

8   And he sent Peter and John, saying, Go and prepare us the passover, that we may eat.

9   And they said unto him, Where wilt thou that we prepare?

10   And he said unto them, Behold, when ye are entered into the city, there shall a man meet you, bearing a pitcher of water; follow him into the house where he entereth in.

11   And ye shall say unto the goodman of the house, The Master saith unto thee, Where is the guestchamber, where I shall eat the passover with my disciples?

12   And he shall shew you a large upper room furnished: there make ready.

13   And they went, and found as he had said unto them: and they made ready the passover.

14   And when the hour was come, he sat down, and the twelve apostles with him.

15   And he said unto them, With desire I have desired to eat this passover with you before I suffer:

16   For I say unto you, I will not any more eat thereof, until it be fulfilled in the kingdom of God.

17   And he took the cup, and gave thanks, and said, Take this, and divide it among yourselves:

18   For I say unto you, I will not drink of the fruit of the vine, until the kingdom of God shall come.

19   And he took bread, and gave thanks, and brake it, and gave unto them, saying, This is my body which is given for you: this do in remembrance of me.

20   Likewise also the cup after supper, saying, This cup is the new testament in my blood, which is shed for you.

21   But, behold, the hand of him that betrayeth me is with me on the table.

22   And truly the Son of man goeth, as it was determined: but woe unto that man by whom he is betrayed!

23   And they began to enquire among themselves, which of them it was that should do this thing.

24 And there was also a strife among them, which of them should be accounted the greatest.

25 And he said unto them, The kings of the Gentiles exercise lordship over them; and they that exercise authority upon them are called benefactors.

26 But ye shall not be so: but he that is greatest among you, let him be as the younger; and he that is chief, as he that doth serve.

27 For whether is greater, he that sitteth at meat, or he that serveth? is not he that sitteth at meat? but I am among you as he that serveth.

28 Ye are they which have continued with me in my temptations.

29 And I appoint unto you a kingdom, as my Father hath appointed unto me;

30 That ye may eat and drink at my table in my kingdom, and sit on thrones judging the twelve tribes of Israel.

31 And the Lord said, Simon, Simon, behold, Satan hath desired to have you, that he may sift you as wheat:

32 But I have prayed for thee, that thy faith fail not: and when thou art converted, strengthen thy brethren.

33 And he said unto him, Lord, I am ready to go with thee, both into prison, and to death.

34 And he said, I tell thee, Peter, the cock shall not crow this day, before that thou shalt thrice deny that thou knowest me.

35 And he said unto them, When I sent you without purse, and scrip, and shoes, lacked ye any thing? And they said, Nothing.

36 Then said he unto them, But now, he that hath a purse, let him take it, and likewise his scrip: and he that hath no sword, let him sell his garment, and buy one.

37 For I say unto you, that this that is written must yet be accomplished in me, And he was reckoned among the transgressors: for the things concerning me have an end.

38 And they said, Lord, behold, here are two swords. And he said unto them, It is enough.

FOLLOWING PAGES:
LEONARDO DA VINCI
The Last Supper
1495-97 (fresco) (post restoration)
Santa Maria della Grazie, Milan, Italy

CHRIST IN THE GARDEN OF GETHSEMANE
Mark 14

32 And they came to a place which was named Gethsemane: and he saith to his disciples, Sit ye here, while I shall pray.

33 And he taketh with him Peter and James and John, and began to be sore amazed, and to be very heavy;

34 And saith unto them, My soul is exceeding sorrowful unto death: tarry ye here, and watch.

35 And he went forward a little, and fell on the ground, and prayed that, if it were possible, the hour might pass from him.

36 And he said, Abba, Father, all things are possible unto thee; take away this cup from me: nevertheless not what I will, but what thou wilt.

37 And he cometh, and findeth them sleeping, and saith unto Peter, Simon, sleepest thou? couldest not thou watch one hour?

38 Watch ye and pray, lest ye enter into temptation. The spirit truly is ready, but the flesh is weak.

39 And again he went away, and prayed, and spake the same words.

40 And when he returned, he found them asleep again, (for their eyes were heavy,) neither wist they what to answer him.

41 And he cometh the third time, and saith unto them, Sleep on now, and take your rest: it is enough, the hour is come; behold, the Son of man is betrayed into the hands of sinners.

SCHAUFELEIN, HANS LEONARD
Christ in Gethsemane
(oil on panel)
Hamburger Kunsthalle, Hamburg, Germany

THE KISS OF JUDAS
Mark 14

42 Rise up, let us go; lo, he that betrayeth me is at hand.

43 And immediately, while he yet spake, cometh Judas, one of the twelve, and with him a great multitude with swords and staves, from the chief priests and the scribes and the elders.

44 And he that betrayed him had given them a token, saying, Whomsoever I shall kiss, that same is he; take him, and lead him away safely.

45 And as soon as he was come, he goeth straightway to him, and saith, Master, master; and kissed him.

46 And they laid their hands on him, and took him.

SALZILLO, FRANCISCO
The Arrest of Christ
detail showing Judas kissing Christ, 1765 (polychrome wood)
Museo Salzillo, Murcia, Spain

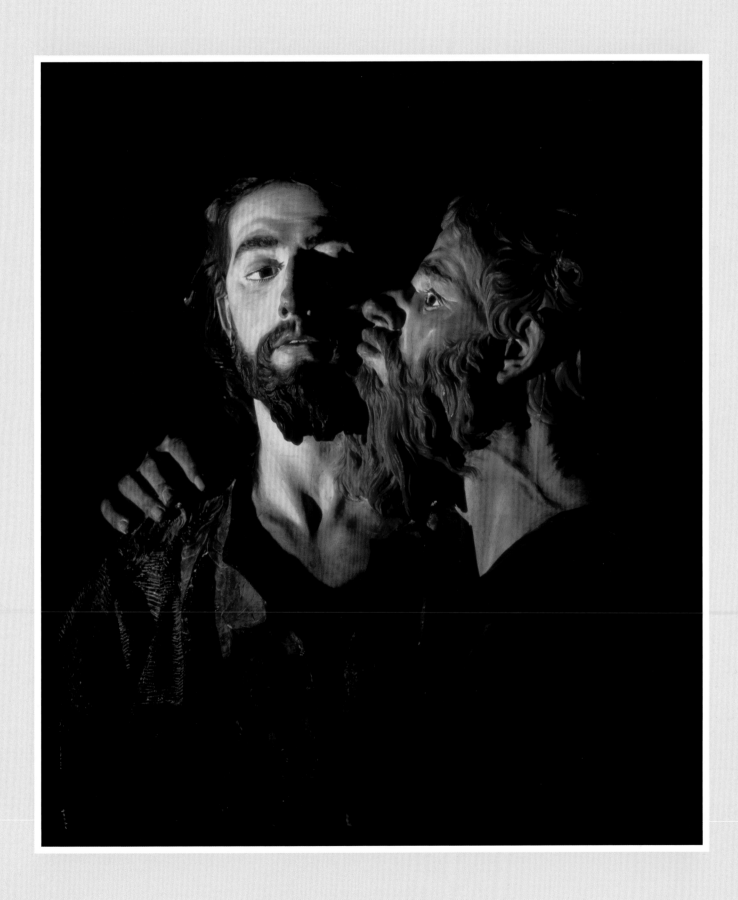

THE ARREST
Mark 14

47 And one of them that stood by drew a sword, and smote a servant of the high priest, and cut off his ear.

48 And Jesus answered and said unto them, Are ye come out, as against a thief, with swords and with staves to take me?

49 I was daily with you in the temple teaching, and ye took me not: but the scriptures must be fulfilled.

50 And they all forsook him, and fled.

51 And there followed him a certain young man, having a linen cloth cast about his naked body; and the young men laid hold on him:

52 And he left the linen cloth, and fled from them naked.

53 And they led Jesus away to the high priest: and with him were assembled all the chief priests and the elders and the scribes.

DYCK, SIR ANTHONY VAN
The Betrayal of Christ
c.1620
Bristol Museums and Art Gallery, Corsham Court, UK

THE FLAGELLATION OF CHRIST

John 18

28 Then led they Jesus from Caiaphas unto the hall of judgment: and it was early; and they themselves went not into the judgment hall, lest they should be defiled; but that they might eat the passover.

29 Pilate then went out unto them, and said, What accusation bring ye against this man?

30 They answered and said unto him, If he were not a malefactor, we would not have delivered him up unto thee.

31 Then said Pilate unto them, Take ye him, and judge him according to your law. The Jews therefore said unto him, It is not lawful for us to put any man to death:

32 That the saying of Jesus might be fulfilled, which he spake, signifying what death he should die.

33 Then Pilate entered into the judgment hall again, and called Jesus, and said unto him, Art thou the King of the Jews?

34 Jesus answered him, Sayest thou this thing of thyself, or did others tell it thee of me?

35 Pilate answered, Am I a Jew? Thine own nation and the chief priests have delivered thee unto me: what hast thou done?

36 Jesus answered, My kingdom is not of this world: if my kingdom were of this world, then would my servants fight, that I should not be delivered to the Jews: but now is my kingdom not from hence.

37 Pilate therefore said unto him, Art thou a king then? Jesus answered, Thou sayest that I am a king. To this end was I born, and for this cause came I into the world, that I should bear witness unto the truth. Every one that is of the truth heareth my voice.

38 Pilate saith unto him, What is truth? And when he had said this, he went out again unto the Jews, and saith unto them, I find in him no fault at all.

39 But ye have a custom, that I should release unto you one at the passover: will ye therefore that I release unto you the King of the Jews?

40 Then cried they all again, saying, Not this man, but Barabbas. Now Barabbas was a robber.

41 Then Pilate therefore took Jesus, and scourged him.

PIERO DELLA FRANCESCA
The Flagellation of Christ
c.1463-4 (tempera on panel)
Galleria Nazionale delle Marche, Urbino, Italy

CHRIST CROWNED WITH THORNS

Matthew 27

27 Then the soldiers of the governor took Jesus into the common hall, and gathered unto him the whole band of soldiers.

28 And they stripped him, and put on him a scarlet robe.

29 And when they had platted a crown of thorns, they put it upon his head, and a reed in his right hand: and they bowed the knee before him, and mocked him, saying, Hail, King of the Jews!

30 And they spit upon him, and took the reed, and smote him on the head.

31 And after that they had mocked him, they took the robe off from him, and put his own raiment on him, and led him away to crucify him.

BOSCH, HIERONYMUS
Christ Mocked (The Crowning with Thorns)
c.1490-1500 (oil on panel)
National Gallery, London, UK

ECCE HOMO
John 19

4   Pilate therefore went forth again, and saith unto them, Behold, I bring him forth to you, that ye may know that I find no fault in him.

5   Then came Jesus forth, wearing the crown of thorns, and the purple robe. And Pilate saith unto them, Behold the man!

6   When the chief priests therefore and officers saw him, they cried out, saying, Crucify him, crucify him. Pilate saith unto them, Take ye him, and crucify him: for I find no fault in him.

7   The Jews answered him, We have a law, and by our law he ought to die, because he made himself the Son of God.

MASSYS, QUENTIN (ATTRIBUTED)
Ecce Homo
1515 (oil on panel)
Prado, Madrid, Spain

ST. PETER WEEPING
Mark 14

66 And as Peter was beneath in the palace, there cometh one of the maids of the high priest:

67 And when she saw Peter warming himself, she looked upon him, and said, And thou also wast with Jesus of Nazareth.

68 But he denied, saying, I know not, neither understand I what thou sayest. And he went out into the porch; and the cock crew.

69 And a maid saw him again, and began to say to them that stood by, This is one of them.

70 And he denied it again. And a little after, they that stood by said again to Peter, Surely thou art one of them: for thou art a Galilaean, and thy speech agreeth thereto.

71 But he began to curse and to swear, saying, I know not this man of whom ye speak.

72 And the second time the cock crew. And Peter called to mind the word that Jesus said unto him, Before the cock crow twice, thou shalt deny me thrice. And when he thought thereon, he wept.

TOUR, GEORGES DE LA (STUDIO OF)
The Tears of St. Peter
(oil on canvas)
Private Collection

THE ROAD TO CALVARY

Luke 23

26 And as they led him away, they laid hold upon one Simon, a Cyrenian, coming out of the country, and on him they laid the cross, that he might bear it after Jesus.

27 And there followed him a great company of people, and of women, which also bewailed and lamented him.

28 But Jesus turning unto them said, Daughters of Jerusalem, weep not for me, but weep for yourselves, and for your children.

29 For, behold, the days are coming, in the which they shall say, Blessed are the barren, and the wombs that never bare, and the paps which never gave suck.

30 Then shall they begin to say to the mountains, Fall on us; and to the hills, Cover us.

31 For if they do these things in a green tree, what shall be done in the dry?

32 And there were also two other, malefactors, led with him to be put to death.

BRUEGHEL, PIETER THE ELDER
The Road to Calvary
1564 (oil on panel)
Kunsthistorisches Museum, Vienna, Austria

THE CRUCIFIXION
Luke 23

33 And when they were come to the place, which is called Calvary, there they crucified him, and the malefactors, one on the right hand, and the other on the left.

34 Then said Jesus, Father, forgive them; for they know not what they do. And they parted his raiment, and cast lots.

35 And the people stood beholding. And the rulers also with them derided him, saying, He saved others; let him save himself, if he be Christ, the chosen of God.

36 And the soldiers also mocked him, coming to him, and offering him vinegar,

37 And saying, If thou be the king of the Jews, save thyself.

38 And a superscription also was written over him in letters of Greek, and Latin, and Hebrew, THIS IS THE KING OF THE JEWS.

39 And one of the malefactors which were hanged railed on him, saying, If thou be Christ, save thyself and us.

40 But the other answering rebuked him, saying, Dost not thou fear God, seeing thou art in the same condemnation?

41 And we indeed justly; for we receive the due reward of our deeds: but this man hath done nothing amiss.

42 And he said unto Jesus, Lord, remember me when thou comest into thy kingdom.

43 And Jesus said unto him, Verily I say unto thee, To day shalt thou be with me in paradise.

44 And it was about the sixth hour, and there was a darkness over all the earth until the ninth hour.

45 And the sun was darkened, and the veil of the temple was rent in the midst.

46 And when Jesus had cried with a loud voice, he said, Father, into thy hands I commend my spirit: and having said thus, he gave up the ghost.

47 Now when the centurion saw what was done, he glorified God, saying, Certainly this was a righteous man.

48 And all the people that came together to that sight, beholding the things which were done, smote their breasts, and returned.

MANTEGNA, ANDREA
Calvary
central predella panel from the St. Zeno of Verona altarpiece, 1456-60 oil on panel
Louvre, Paris, France

THE DEPOSITION
John 19

33 But when they came to Jesus, and saw that he was dead already, they brake not his legs:

34 But one of the soldiers with a spear pierced his side, and forthwith came there out blood and water.

35 And he that saw it bare record, and his record is true: and he knoweth that he saith true, that ye might believe.

36 For these things were done, that the scripture should be fulfilled, A bone of him shall not be broken.

37 And again another scripture saith, They shall look on him whom they pierced.

38 And after this Joseph of Arimathaea, being a disciple of Jesus, but secretly for fear of the Jews, besought Pilate that he might take away the body of Jesus: and Pilate gave him leave. He came therefore, and took the body of Jesus.

39 And there came also Nicodemus, which at the first came to Jesus by night, and brought a mixture of myrrh and aloes, about an hundred pound weight.

40 Then took they the body of Jesus, and wound it in linen clothes with the spices, as the manner of the Jews is to bury.

41 Now in the place where he was crucified there was a garden; and in the garden a new sepulchre, wherein was never man yet laid.

42 There laid they Jesus therefore because of the Jews' preparation day; for the sepulchre was nigh at hand.

POUSSIN, NICOLAS
The Deposition
c.1630 (oil on canvas)
Hermitage, St. Petersburg, Russia

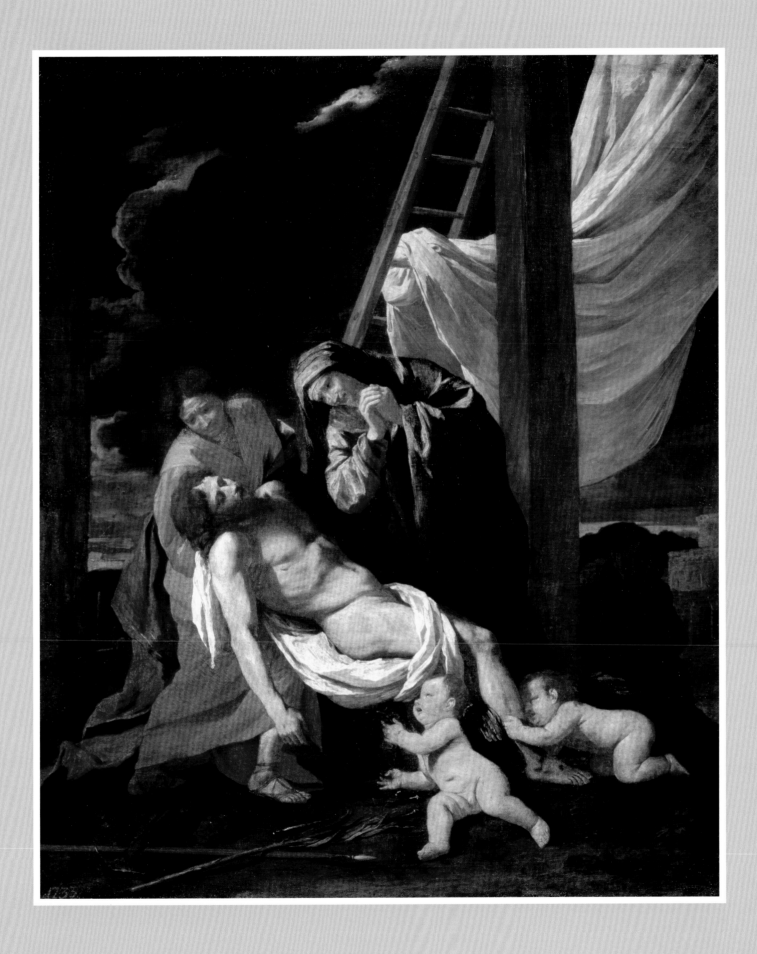

THE ENTOMBMENT
Luke 23

49 And all his acquaintance, and the women that followed him from Galilee, stood afar off, beholding these things.

50 And, behold, there was a man named Joseph, a counsellor; and he was a good man, and a just:

51 (The same had not consented to the counsel and deed of them;) he was of Arimathaea, a city of the Jews: who also himself waited for the kingdom of God.

52 This man went unto Pilate, and begged the body of Jesus.

53 And he took it down, and wrapped it in linen, and laid it in a sepulchre that was hewn in stone, wherein never man before was laid.

54 And that day was the preparation, and the sabbath drew on.

55 And the women also, which came with him from Galilee, followed after, and beheld the sepulchre, and how his body was laid.

56 And they returned, and prepared spices and ointments; and rested the sabbath day according to the commandment.

WEYDEN, ROGIER VAN DER
The Entombment
c.1450 (oil on panel)
Galleria degli Uffizi, Florence, Italy

THE RESURRECTION
Luke 18

31 Then he took unto him the twelve, and said unto them, Behold, we go up to Jerusalem, and all things that are written by the prophets concerning the Son of man shall be accomplished.

32 For he shall be delivered unto the Gentiles, and shall be mocked, and spitefully entreated, and spitted on:

33 And they shall scourge him, and put him to death: and the third day he shall rise again.

34 And they understood none of these things: and this saying was hid from them, neither knew they the things which were spoken.

PIERO DELLA FRANCESCA,
The Resurrection
c.1463 (fresco)
Pinacoteca, Sansepolcro, Italy

CHRIST APPEARING TO MARY MAGDALENE

John 20

11 But Mary stood without at the sepulchre weeping: and as she wept, she stooped down, and looked into the sepulchre,

12 And seeth two angels in white sitting, the one at the head, and the other at the feet, where the body of Jesus had lain.

13 And they say unto her, Woman, why weepest thou? She saith unto them, Because they have taken away my Lord, and I know not where they have laid him.

14 And when she had thus said, she turned herself back, and saw Jesus standing, and knew not that it was Jesus.

15 Jesus saith unto her, Woman, why weepest thou? whom seekest thou? She, supposing him to be the gardener, saith unto him, Sir, if thou have borne him hence, tell me where thou hast laid him, and I will take him away.

16 Jesus saith unto her, Mary. She turned herself, and saith unto him, Rabboni; which is to say, Master.

17 Jesus saith unto her, Touch me not; for I am not yet ascended to my Father: but go to my brethren, and say unto them, I ascend unto my Father, and your Father; and to my God, and your God.

18 Mary Magdalene came and told the disciples that she had seen the Lord, and that he had spoken these things unto her.

RYDER, ALBERT PINKHAM
Christ Appearing to Mary
Smithsonian Institution, Washington DC

CHRIST APPEARING ON THE ROAD TO EMMAUS

Luke 24

13 And, behold, two of them went that same day to a village called Emmaus, which was from Jerusalem about threescore furlongs.

14 And they talked together of all these things which had happened.

15 And it came to pass, that, while they communed together and reasoned, Jesus himself drew near, and went with them.

16 But their eyes were holden that they should not know him.

17 And he said unto them, What manner of communications are these that ye have one to another, as ye walk, and are sad?

18 And the one of them, whose name was Cleopas, answering said unto him, Art thou only a stranger in Jerusalem, and hast not known the things which are come to pass there in these days?

19 And he said unto them, What things? And they said unto him, Concerning Jesus of Nazareth, which was a prophet mighty in deed and word before God and all the people:

20 And how the chief priests and our rulers delivered him to be condemned to death, and have crucified him.

21 But we trusted that it had been he which should have redeemed Israel: and beside all this, to day is the third day since these things were done.

22 Yea, and certain women also of our company made us astonished, which were early at the sepulchre;

23 And when they found not his body, they came, saying, that they had also seen a vision of angels, which said that he was alive.

24 And certain of them which were with us went to the sepulchre, and found it even so as the women had said: but him they saw not.

25 Then he said unto them, O fools, and slow of heart to believe all that the prophets have spoken:

26 Ought not Christ to have suffered these things, and to enter into his glory?

27 And beginning at Moses and all the prophets, he expounded unto them in all the scriptures the things concerning himself.

28 And they drew nigh unto the village, whither they went: and he made as though he would have gone further.

29 But they constrained him, saying, Abide with us: for it is toward evening, and the day is far spent. And he went in to tarry with them.

30 And it came to pass, as he sat at meat with them, he took bread, and blessed it, and brake, and gave to them.

31 And their eyes were opened, and they knew him; and he vanished out of their sight.

32 And they said one to another, Did not our heart burn within us, while he talked with us by the way, and while he opened to us the scriptures?

DUCCIO DI BUONINSEGNA
Christ Appearing on the Road to Emmaus
1308-11
Museo dell'Opera del Duomo, Siena, Italy

TITIAN (TIZIANO VECELLIO)
The Supper at Emmaus
c.1535 (oil on canvas)
Louvre, Paris, France

The Incredulity of St. Thomas

John 20

19 Then the same day at evening, being the first day of the week, when the doors were shut where the disciples were assembled for fear of the Jews, came Jesus and stood in the midst, and saith unto them, Peace be unto you.

20 And when he had so said, he shewed unto them his hands and his side. Then were the disciples glad, when they saw the Lord.

21 Then said Jesus to them again, Peace be unto you: as my Father hath sent me, even so send I you.

22 And when he had said this, he breathed on them, and saith unto them, Receive ye the Holy Ghost:

23 Whose soever sins ye remit, they are remitted unto them; and whose soever sins ye retain, they are retained.

24 But Thomas, one of the twelve, called Didymus, was not with them when Jesus came.

25 The other disciples therefore said unto him, We have seen the Lord. But he said unto them, Except I shall see in his hands the print of the nails, and put my finger into the print of the nails, and thrust my hand into his side, I will not believe.

26 And after eight days again his disciples were within, and Thomas with them: then came Jesus, the doors being shut, and stood in the midst, and said, Peace be unto you.

27 Then saith he to Thomas, Reach hither thy finger, and behold my hands; and reach hither thy hand, and thrust it into my side: and be not faithless, but believing.

28 And Thomas answered and said unto him, My Lord and my God.

29 Jesus saith unto him, Thomas, because thou hast seen me, thou hast believed: blessed are they that have not seen, and yet have believed.

CARAVAGGIO, MICHELANGELO MERISI DA
The Incredulity of St. Thomas
1602-03 (oil on canvas)
Schloss Sanssouci, Potsdam, Germany

THE MIRACULOUS DRAUGHT OF FISHES

John 21

1 After these things Jesus shewed himself again to the disciples at the sea of Tiberias; and on this wise shewed he himself.

2 There were together Simon Peter, and Thomas called Didymus, and Nathanael of Cana in Galilee, and the sons of Zebedee, and two other of his disciples.

3 Simon Peter saith unto them, I go a fishing. They say unto him, We also go with thee. They went forth, and entered into a ship immediately; and that night they caught nothing.

4 But when the morning was now come, Jesus stood on the shore: but the disciples knew not that it was Jesus.

5 Then Jesus saith unto them, Children, have ye any meat? They answered him, No.

6 And he said unto them, Cast the net on the right side of the ship, and ye shall find. They cast therefore, and now they were not able to draw it for the multitude of fishes.

7 Therefore that disciple whom Jesus loved saith unto Peter, It is the Lord. Now when Simon Peter heard that it was the Lord, he girt his fisher's coat unto him, (for he was naked,) and did cast himself into the sea.

8 And the other disciples came in a little ship; (for they were not far from land, but as it were two hundred cubits,) dragging the net with fishes.

9 As soon then as they were come to land, they saw a fire of coals there, and fish laid thereon, and bread.

10 Jesus saith unto them, Bring of the fish which ye have now caught.

11 Simon Peter went up, and drew the net to land full of great fishes, an hundred and fifty and three: and for all there were so many, yet was not the net broken.

12 Jesus saith unto them, Come and dine. And none of the disciples durst ask him, Who art thou? knowing that it was the Lord.

13 Jesus then cometh, and taketh bread, and giveth them, and fish likewise.

14 This is now the third time that Jesus shewed himself to his disciples, after that he was risen from the dead.

WITZ, KONRAD
Miraculous Draught of Fishes
from the Altarpiece of Cardinal Francois de Mies, c.1444 (oil on panel)
Musée d'Art et d'Histoire, Geneva, Switzerland

THE ASCENSION OF CHRIST

Mark 16

14 Afterward he appeared unto the eleven as they sat at meat, and upbraided them with their unbelief and hardness of heart, because they believed not them which had seen him after he was risen.

15 And he said unto them, Go ye into all the world, and preach the gospel to every creature.

16 He that believeth and is baptized shall be saved; but he that believeth not shall be damned.

17 And these signs shall follow them that believe; In my name shall they cast out devils; they shall speak with new tongues;

18 They shall take up serpents; and if they drink any deadly thing, it shall not hurt them; they shall lay hands on the sick, and they shall recover.

19 So then after the Lord had spoken unto them, he was received up into heaven, and sat on the right hand of God.

20 And they went forth, and preached every where, the Lord working with them, and confirming the word with signs following. Amen.

PERUGINO, PIETRO
The Ascension of Christ
1495-98 (oil on panel)
Musée des Beaux-Arts, Lyon, France

The Last Judgement
Revelation 20

1 And I saw an angel come down from heaven, having the key of the bottomless pit and a great chain in his hand.

2 And he laid hold on the dragon, that old serpent, which is the Devil, and Satan, and bound him a thousand years,

3 And cast him into the bottomless pit, and shut him up, and set a seal upon him, that he should deceive the nations no more, till the thousand years should be fulfilled: and after that he must be loosed a little season.

4 And I saw thrones, and they sat upon them, and judgment was given unto them: and I saw the souls of them that were beheaded for the witness of Jesus, and for the word of God, and which had not worshipped the beast, neither his image, neither had received his mark upon their foreheads, or in their hands; and they lived and reigned with Christ a thousand years.

5 But the rest of the dead lived not again until the thousand years were finished. This is the first resurrection.

6 Blessed and holy is he that hath part in the first resurrection: on such the second death hath no power, but they shall be priests of God and of Christ, and shall reign with him a thousand years.

7 And when the thousand years are expired, Satan shall be loosed out of his prison,

8 And shall go out to deceive the nations which are in the four quarters of the earth, Gog, and Magog, to gather them together to battle: the number of whom is as the sand of the sea.

9 And they went up on the breadth of the earth, and compassed the camp of the saints about, and the beloved city: and fire came down from God out of heaven, and devoured them.

10 And the devil that deceived them was cast into the lake of fire and brimstone, where the beast and the false prophet are, and shall be tormented day and night for ever and ever.

11 And I saw a great white throne, and him that sat on it, from whose face the earth and the heaven fled away; and there was found no place for them.

12 And I saw the dead, small and great, stand before God; and the books were opened: and another book was opened, which is the book of life: and the dead were judged out of those things which were written in the books, according to their works.

13 And the sea gave up the dead which were in it; and death and hell delivered up the dead which were in them: and they were judged every man according to their works.

14 And death and hell were cast into the lake of fire. This is the second death.

15 And whosoever was not found written in the book of life was cast into the lake of fire.

MICHELANGELO
Last Judgement
from the Sistine Chapel, 1538-41 (fresco)
Vatican Museums and Galleries, Vatican City, Italy